M. C Briggs

Regress and slavery versus Progress and Poverty

M. C Briggs

Regress and slavery versus Progress and Poverty

ISBN/EAN: 9783744799355

Printed in Europe, USA, Canada, Australia, Japan

Cover: Foto ©Suzi / pixelio.de

More available books at **www.hansebooks.com**

Regress and Slavery

vs.

"Progress and Poverty"

By M. C. Briggs

THE SINGLE-TAX THEORY SHOWN TO BE UNJUST, IMPRACTICABLE, AND ABSURD

NEW YORK
PRINTED BY HUNT & EATON
150 Fifth Avenue
1891

REGRESS AND SLAVERY

VS.

"PROGRESS AND POVERTY."

FIRST PAPER.

A BAD book by a bad man is bad. A bad book by a good man is very bad. The known virtues of the author yield sanction and support to his errors.

A good man may write a bad book because of unconscious bias, or a tangential impulse thrown into his early life, or the lack of special knowledge lying outside of his large general intelligence, in which case his mistakes are dangerously commended by his own known information and integrity. Goethe says, "Nothing is more terrible than active ignorance." Had he added amiable and (if the reader can pardon the surface contradiction) intelligent ignorance, the sentence would have been philosophically complete.

Mr. Henry George has given to the world a work entitled *Progress and Poverty*. It is honest, labored, earnest, fallacious, audacious, able in its way, impracticable, misleading, mischievous. Hundreds have read it, and thousands from them catch and echo fragments and fancies, often to the detriment of the author, and always to the damagement of truth. With perfect respect for the writer, I propose to review the book, putting facts into the witness-box and trying the case before the court of common sense. *Facta sunt potentiora verbis.*

Progress creates new wants. New wants induce new industries and new methods of old industries.

That growth of science, art, invention, enlightenment, and civil order which we fondly call progressive civilization, by adding efficiency to labor and offering new opportunities and incentives to invention, constantly deranges existing relations and necessitates redistribution of workers with hand and brain.

Thus greatly improved agricultural and mechanical machinery enables one to do to-day as much as ten or twenty did in the yesterdays. Consequently, nine or nineteen are thrown out of employment, and the relative number of tillers of the soil or toilers in the shop is correspondingly lessened. Many of us not yet bowed with the weight of incumbent years recall those simpler times when a large proportion of our people were small farmers, and the hoe and the single plow, the hand-rake and the sickle, the cradle and the mower's scythe furnished food for man and beast. In these better days farming, though not exempt from the sweat of labor, is well-nigh exalted to a fine art. But what is to be done with the released hands?

Wives and daughters younger than Sojourner Truth remember when their grandmothers and mothers seeded the cotton, carded and spun the wool, drew flaxen threads from the whirring wheel, and stitched home-made garments for rosy girls and boys. These homely pursuits have given place to machinery and the skill of experts. But where shall scope be found for the disengaged?

The tallow-dip yields to oil, oil to gas, and gas to lightning; naked floors hide their rude simplicity under tapestry fit for kings, and the honest old wash-tub surrenders at discretion to an upstart laundry which returns your soiled linen, washed, dried, and ironed in thirteen minutes by the watch. The ox-cart creaks no more, and the old-time stage-coach stares abashed at the thundering trains which run without weariness and puff without fainting. The telegraph distances sunlight, and men whisper their love by telephone to ears half a thousand miles away. If life be measured by what is put into it, there are men living this blessed morning a thousand years older than Methuselah would have been if he had haunted this mundane orb nine hundred and sixty-nine years longer.

All these beneficent changes, each in its own order and degree, bring temporary confusion.

They disturb the industrial balance and cause class to jostle class, and make men think themselves victims of human injustice when they are only subjects of irrepealable and uplifting law.

It is thus that progress works revolutions which leave in their wake considerable numbers of unemployed, bewildered, discouraged, and possibly embittered men, who lend open ears to the glib self-styled reformers, too often without discriminating between the authentic and the spurious. To this list of worthy persons must be added far less deserving classes, such as the supine and thriftless, the indifferent and dishonest, the thousands impoverished by their own vices, the alarming influx into our cities of a low class of foreigners, utopian dreamers, impracticable sporadists to whom every thing old is evil, political bummers, and the general riffraff whose lives run all to ears and stomach. Altogether they present a formidable array, ever eager to hear of a patent remedy for their ills, the more gorgeously unreasonable the better.

To this immense miscellany of humanity some recent authors have addressed themselves with flattering success. To the religiously unsettled *Robert Elsmere* offers

> " A balm for every wound,
> A cordial for [their] fears."

To the industrially unsettled Bellamy's thin but glittering dream and Henry George's *Progress and Poverty* are as water to a thirsty soul. Let honesty shield me from suspicion of unamiability when I aver that the lucrative welcome given to these three most fallacious books of the day is startling proof of the enfeeblement of popular reason by the avalanche of gushy, illogical, unphilosophical, half-lunatic literature which stocks our public libraries and burdens the center-tables of our homes.

Time is too valuable to be expended upon the ideal commonwealths of earlier dates, such as Plato's *Republic*, Moore's *Utopia*, Bacon's *New Altantis*, and Campanella's *Civitas Solis*. Nor is it worth while to linger upon that brilliant phantasmagoria, *Looking Backward*.

Progress and Poverty is an earnest work, written by an honest man with serious intent. To that, therefore, as containing all the tangible reasons and no reasons of the wide and wild speculation, this review will be confined.

Mr. George makes much account of certain nice definitions, with respect to which he rather boastfully differs from other writers on political economy, such as the difference between capital and wealth, paper money and wealth, paper money and capital, capital and land, interest and revenue, the exact meaning of wages, the law of wages, wages and interest, the source of wages, etc., etc. These definitions and distinctions are doubtless interesting to verbalistic political economists, but, practically, most of them are of no more value to economic life than an assumed difference between sunshine and sunbeams, air and atmosphere, water and protoxide of hydrogen. The actual affairs of life move on as regularly and lawfully without as with them, as is abundantly proved by the fact that ninety-nine hundredths of the best practical political economists know

nothing of the refined technics of the book.   I
infer that Mr. George himself attaches no im-
portance to his improved terminology outside
of its imagined bearing upon the main idea.
His revised terms are expletives used to help
us up to the single-tax theory, which is the
soul and substance of the entire work.   If the
book fails to bring its readers to an acceptance
of that theory he will regard it as a failure indeed.   I shall be pardoned, therefore, if, like a
Yankee, I take a short cut and go directly to
the theory of exclusive land taxation, which
is the apple of his eye.   If that can be shown
to be unjust, impracticable, and absurd, it would
be superfluous to examine in detail the argument by which it is supported.   Robert Hall
said, " One need not eat a whole flitch of bacon
to learn whether it is tainted."

SECOND PAPER.

IT is no more than just that one who advances a theory should be permitted to state it for himself.   After rejecting all the cures for life's ills heretofore propounded Mr. George gives what he confidently names " THE TRUE REMEDY."   Beginning with the oft-repeated proposition that "land is the source of all wealth" (p. 45), and assuming that industrial depressions, financial crises, poverty, ignorance, anarchy, degradation, vice, and crime all result primarily, chiefly, and necessarily from private ownership of land, he proceeds to say the following things:

Page 295: "We have traced the unequal distribution of wealth, which is the curse and menace of modern civilization, to the institution of private property in land.   We have seen that as long as this institution exists no increase of productive power can permanently benefit the masses, but, on the contrary, must tend still further to depress their condition. We have examined all the remedies short of the abolition of private property in land which are currently relied on or proposed for the relief of poverty and the better distribution of wealth, and have found them all inefficacious or impracticable. . . . To extirpate poverty, to make wages what justice commands they should be—the full earnings of the laborer—we must therefore substitute for the individual ownership of land a common ownership. Nothing else will go to the cause of the evil; in nothing else is there the slightest hope. This, then, is the remedy for the unjust and unequal distribution of wealth apparent in modern civilization and for all the evils which flow from it. *We must make land common property.*"

Page 303: "Whatever may be said for the institution of private property in land, it is therefore plain that it cannot be defended on the score of justice."

Page 321: "Private ownership of land is the

nether millstone. Material progress is the upper millstone. Between them, with an increasing pressure, the working classes are being ground."

Page 304: " There is on earth no power which can rightfully make a grant of private ownership in land. . . . Let the parchments be ever so many, or possession ever so long, nature and justice can recognize no right in one man to the possession and enjoyment of land that is not equally the right of all his fellows."

Page 305 : " The wide-spreading social evils which every-where oppress men amid advancing civilization spring from a great primary wrong—the appropriation, as the exclusive property of some men, of the land on which and from which all must live. From this fundamental injustice flow all the injustices which distort and endanger modern development, which condemn the producer of wealth to poverty and pamper the non-producer in luxury, which rear the tenement-house with the palace, plant the brothel behind the church, and compel us to build prisons as we open new schools."

Pages 307, 308: "To improvements such an original title can be shown; but it is a title only to the improvements, and not to the land itself. If I clear a forest, drain a swamp, or fill a morass, all I can justly claim is the value given by these exertions. They give me no right to the land itself, no claim other than to my equal share with every other member of the community in the value which is added to it by the growth of the community. But it will be said there are improvements which in time become indistinguishable from the land itself. Very well; then the title to the improvements becomes blended with the title to the land; the individual right is lost in the common right. . . . Thus the value of land expresses in exact and tangible form the right of the community in land held by an individual; and rent expresses the exact amount which the individual should pay to the community to satisfy the equal rights of all other members of the community. Thus if we concede to priority of possession the undisturbed use of land, confiscating rent for the benefit of the community, we reconcile the fixity of tenure which is necessary for improvement with a full and complete recognition of the equal rights of all to the use of land."

Mr. George claims that the government might rightly and righteously assume title to all land without a thought of compensating those who have purchased it from that same government. In opposing the plan of compensation advocated by Herbert Spencer and John Stuart Mill he delivers himself with refreshing freedom. Thus on pages 326–328, " By the time the people of any such country as England or the United States are sufficiently aroused to the injustice and disadvantages of individual ownership of land to induce them to attempt its nationalization, they will be sufficiently aroused to nationalize it in a much more direct and easy way than by purchase. They will not trouble themselves about compensating the proprietors of land. . . . If the land of any country belongs to the people of that country, what right, in morality and justice, have the individuals called land-owners to the rent? . . . Why not make short work of the matter anyhow?"

Mr. George shows occasional symptoms of a fear that the "shock" of so unique a revolution might prove inconveniently severe. Read him on pages 362–364:

"We have weighed every objection, and seen that neither on the ground of equity nor expediency is there any thing to deter us from making the land common property by confiscation. But the question of method remains. We should satisfy the laws of justice, we should meet all economic requirements by at one stroke abolishing all private titles, declaring all land public property, and letting it out to the highest bidder in lots to suit, under such conditions as would sacredly guard the private right to improvements. . . . But such a plan, though perfectly feasible, does not seem to me the best. Or, rather, I propose to accomplish the same thing in a simpler, easier, and quieter way than that of formally confis-

cating all the land and formally letting it out
to the highest bidder. To do that would
involve a needless shock to present customs
and habits of thought, which is to be avoided.
To do that would involve a needless exten-
sion of governmental machinery, which is to
be avoided. . . . I do not propose either to
purchase or to confiscate private property in
land. The first would be unjust, the second
needless. Let the individuals who now hold
it still retain, if they want to, possession of
what they are pleased to call *their* land. Let
them continue to call it *their* land. Let them
buy and sell, and bequeath and devise it.
We may safely leave them the shell if we take
the kernel. *It is not necessary to confiscate the
land ; it is only necessary to confiscate rent.* . . .
We already take some rent in taxation. We
have only to make some changes in our mode
of taxation to take it all. What I therefore
propose is the simple yet sovereign remedy,
which is to raise wages, increase the earnings
of capital, extirpate pauperism, abolish poverty, give lucrative employment to whoever

2

wishes it, afford free scope to human powers, lessen crime, elevate morals and taste and intelligence, purify government, and carry civilization to yet nobler heights, is—*to appropriate rent by taxation.* In this way the State may become the universal landlord without calling herself so, and without assuming a single new function. In form the ownership of land would remain as now. No owner of land need be dispossessed, and no restriction need be placed upon the amount of land any one could hold. For rent being taken by the State in taxes, land, no matter in whose name it stood, would be really common property, and every member of the community would participate in the advantages of its ownership. Now, as the taxation of rent or land values must necessarily be increased just as we abolish other taxes, we may put the proposition into practical form by proposing *to abolish all taxes save that upon land.*"

Such is the theory of the "single tax." The State must own the land, the land must pay its full rental value in taxes to the "community" or "the State," all other forms of wealth to remain forever untaxed.

If the gifted author would kindly tell us whom this majestic "we" represents—what parties are comprehended under that capacious pronoun which vaults lightly over obstacles which thinking men must see to be insuperable under our form of government, and deprecable and despicable under any form, he would do us a kindness. Community, too, as used by him, needs a severer definition. If "we" are to take the "kernel," precisely what members of the national family are to enjoy that luxury? The "we" that takes some, and modestly proposes to take all, ought to disclothe itself of all ambiguity, and give the poor "hayseeds" a fair look at the mouth which is to swallow them.

Soberly, so full a statement of the single-tax fancy has been given, first, that the author may be justly dealt with; second, that all may know what it is; third, that it may refute itself.

THIRD PAPER.

IN the problem under view there are so many elements which, for the sake of such readers as have not found special occasion to think on such themes, it may be profitable to set in order.

1. One of the broad fallacies which under-gird the scheme of *Progress and Poverty* is *the assumption that wealth inheres in and springs spontaneously from the land.*

There is no more wealth in land itself and alone than in electricity, gravitation, or moon-light. Wealth, in all its comforts, comple-ments, and combinations, shapes and shades, moods and tenses, is the product of thought-directed energy. It is a product of mind. In any and every sense above the nakedest ani-mal existence, in regions where spontaneous growths fill human stomachs—if even there an exception should be conceded—wealth is the product of thinking toilfully.

Thus two men enter alike on lands of equal fertility, with equal strength and opportunities. One grows rich and influential ; the other remains as poor as the turkey which tradition declares followed Job through his fallen fortunes. Stanley traversed millions of acres of land as fat as Eden, clothed with forests of valuable timber, beautified by crystal streams, in sight of mountains rich in minerals, yet trodden for indefinite ages by naked and comfortless savages. Digger Indians owned the rivers and mountains of California long enough before keener eyes detected the witching glitter that set the world agog. The rich and the poor, the thrifty and the thriftless, the moral and the impure, the noble and the ignoble, are found side by side among owners and tillers of the soil.

2. *The book appears to ignore the vital similarity in fundamental conditions between the products of commerce and mechanical skill and the fruits of agricultural and horticultural toil.*

Two young men set out in life together. One chooses mechanics and the other takes to farm life. If one lounges idly in his shop, and the other will not plow by reason of the cold, both will beg in harvest and have nothing. But let the one improve his skill and ply his tools, and the other clear, fence, underdrain, plow, sow, reap, and, by exchanges mutually profitable, both will have bread enough and to spare. Where lies the fundamental difference between them, as to the rightfulness of private ownership? One builds a shop and makes tables, say. Practically the trade is of no value without the shop, the shop is of no value without material and tools, the tools and material are of no value without industrial use. The other buys honest acres from " the State," erects buildings, constructs fences, purchases implements. Practically the land is valueless without fences and buildings, fences and buildings are valueless without implements, implements are valueless without industrial use. Which of the two has the superior right to the safety and satisfaction of private ownership? The results in both cases are products of thoughtful industry.

"No, no," says *Progress and Poverty*. "The mechanic *makes* his wealth; the farmer's *grows*." Did the mechanic make the timber and the iron, and the marble and the brass, and the glue-stock and the coal? "No, but he adapted the material to convenient uses." Exactly; and how came -the farmer's crops? Did they grow up some dark morn like Topsy, all of themselves? Which employed most and hardest toil? Between the two the farmer has had more work and more care. Is it, then, in their mutual dependency to be a common ownership throughout? "O, never," says *Progress and Poverty*. "The farmer has no right or partnership interest in the mechanic's shop and tools and tables; but the mechanic has as much and as many rights in the farmer's farm as the farmer himself has."

But the improvements belong to the farmer. The building, the hedges, the subsoiling, the under-drainage, the cellars, the wells, the orchards, the vineyards, the asparagus-beds, the seeded timothy meadows and wide clover fields belong to John the farmer, and Jim the mechanic is so far shut out by undisputed private ownership.

Wrong again. If " there are improvements which in time become indistinguishable (or inseparable) from the land, . . . then the title to the improvements becomes blended with the title to the land; the individual right is lost in the common right." And John, after his years of hard labor and weary waiting, must try to console himself with the reflection that he and the laziest tramp alike have a sixty-five millionth interest in the " common ownership " of that farm and its " indistinguishable " improvements.   He will surely be content with that !

Mr. George would urge that the justice of this one-sided arrangement arises from the fact that it is the growth of community that adds value to land, whether the land be used to supply the sumptuary market or for city lots ; and therefore the community has a right to the increase of value dependent on the growth of population.

But is land the only thing the value of which is enhanced by the increase of inhabitants?

Let us see.   A man builds a store, shop, mill,
elevator, railroad, theater, school-house, upon
an uninhabited plain.   What is the value of
these products of labor?   They are worthless.
The land, being less destructible and more
capable of yielding food to the owner, is less
dependent than other species of property upon
community.   Indeed, the great increase of
value of land in a populous city results from
the fact that population so greatly enhances
the value of stores, offices, shops, mills, banks,
theaters, etc., erected upon it.   The land
shares but moderately and by consequence in
the greatly improved opportunities brought to
commerce, manufacture, exchange, and art, by
large and contiguous numbers of patrons.   So
great are these advantages to multiform enterprises that men find it more profitable to rent
the land than to purchase it, as capital brings
quicker and larger returns invested in trade
than in the ground on which the palaces of
trade stand.   A lot on Broadway, New York,
is worth three thousand dollars a front foot,
and rents for fifty thousand a year ; but an

eight-story building on it accommodates a business which yields an income of a million a year. Where then is the justice of taxing the landlord to pay for governmental protection and opportunities to enrich the lessee? And where is the equity of wresting from the lot-owner the full rental value while the man who grows rich upon it pays nothing? Thus the unlucky owner is robbed both of ownership and of rent, and left with only the care of an estate, which he must manage without so much as the compensation of a hireling.

"But you do not get the whole case," says *Progress and Poverty.* "Let the individuals who hold it still retain, if they want to, possession of what they are pleased to call *their* land. Let them buy and sell and bequeath and devise it," and of course cultivate and use it in their own way.

What now! Has the snake swallowed itself? Has the prudence which seeks to avoid "shocks" taken the spinal marrow out of the "True Remedy?" If no limit is to be set to the area which one may hold, and the holder may buy, sell, bequeath, and devise, where is the relief to the laboring classes? Tax the holder the full rental value, and you force upon him the strongest motive to cut down the wages of his hired help. Either he must be content to toil for a mere and precarious living—precarious because of the uncertainty of seasons, crops, and markets—or abandon the land to the grasp and greed of a robber government, or reduce the expense of production to the lowest possible figure. Thus the "True Remedy" reaches a lame and impotent conclusion which retains all the possible evils of private ownership, with a greatly aggravated incentive to oppress the hireling in his wages. How such an arrangement is to " increase wages, extirpate pauperism, abolish poverty, lessen crime, elevate morals, purify government, and carry civilization to yet nobler heights," is one of the puzzles which must be relegated to minds of abnormal cast. To carry such a scheme into effect it would be necessary to extend the functions of the contemplated paternal government to all the minutiæ of tillage and land management, and appoint a supervising and enforcing functionary for every hundred or two of husbandmen.

FOURTH PAPER.

3. In advocating his scheme of exclusive land taxation Mr. George appears *strangely incognizant of the ground-reasons by which taxation must be justified.* To maintain order, protect the individual in his person, pursuits, and possessions, and provide public institutions for the general good are the objects of government and the prime conditions of progressive civilization. To maintain government for such ends all right-minded citizens are willing to be equitably taxed. They regard money paid in reasonable taxes as a wise and profitable investment. Even a bad government is better than none, and a good one is a priceless boon to all who live peacefully under its sway. And when a government provides in its structural plan peaceable remedies, such as free speech, a free press, a free forum, a free pulpit, and a free ballot, for real or fancied

evils, an attempt at violent and treasonable overthrow is beyond the reach of possible extenuation. To tax a people in a just way for the maintenance of a just and wholesome representative government is a policy so obviously wise and necessary that dissidents imperil their reputation for candor and common sense by declaiming against it. But the tax must be levied upon all who need protection. The landowner needs it to guarantee and defend his title and assure him the peaceable enjoyment of the fruits of his toil. Very quickly does feeble and capricious government show itself in neglected, half-tilled, and abandoned farms. In parts of Central America I have seen miles on miles of abandoned ranches. There are the cactus hedges, the long avenues of stately flowering trees, and the hacienda buildings in various stages of decay, where the soil is exhaustlessly fertile and the fructifying sun quickens every seed committed to the ground. Bad government is the explanation. The people are thriftless because unconfident. Enterprise is discouraged, and uncertainty hangs like a pall upon the spirits of men.

But if the land-owner needs the strong arm of the State, the merchant, the manufacturer, the banker, the ship-master need it still more. Mr. George will not consent to call bonds and greenbacks capital; but, name as you will, they shrink to nothingness under a constantly alarming prospect of revolution. Had our " erring brothers " of the South achieved a final triumph our bonds would have been as worthless as Confederate notes are to-day. And all other kinds of wealth and capital shrink and shrivel under the same law. Why then should the land-owner pay for the protection of the ship-master, merchant, manufacturer, broker, bond-holder? Even-handed justice requires that all who are assured by and dependent on civil stability and protection should help to pay for them.

Land-owners are at this date bending under burdens which threaten to crush them. Agriculture is depressed. Owners of city lots— less affected than tillers—in our new cities are struggling under heavy taxes for improvements. The single-tax scheme would leave them all helplessly and hopelessly poor. Land-ownership or occupancy would be shunned as an irritating and profitless thing. All other ventures and investments would be crowded to suffocation. Production would fall below the demands of consumption, and starvation look in at all doors, unless government should be clothed with power to compel a sufficient number, like serfs of the soil, to plow and sow that non-producers might eat and live.

If the needs of individual life and private business justify general taxation there are public institutions, such as common schools, highways, bridges, court-houses, asylums, which are of contingent interest to every member of the body politic, and yet can be supported only by governmental outlay of funds supplied by taxation. Interests so common imply a common obligation. The amount levied under a fair system to support a good government is inconsiderable compared with the advantages it affords.

4. *Progress and Poverty* wholly ignores a most important and beneficent fact in the industrial problem, namely, *That the causes which lessen the relative demand for hands in one industry are features of a wide general sweep of progress which creates new industries faster than the old are overstocked or supplanted.*

Thus, if petroleum displaces whale-oil, the petroleum industry needs more men than are dismissed from the whalers. If gas dims the light of petroleum, it also offers employment compensative of the loss in the superseded work. Electricity in its turn supersedes gas, and thousands find use for themselves in that ever-growing necessity of economic life. Increasing wealth opens doors of profitable opportunity for improved architecture and decorative art. A log-cabin for the pioneer could be built by five men in a day or two. The affluent " settler " moves out of the log-house into a building which requires ten men for ten months in the building, and possibly as many more to furnish and decorate. Affluence and taste must needs be gratified with

3

paintings, statuary, and music, and the ground, erst adorned with corn and cabbages, now blushes with every shape and shade of beauty under the gardener's skill. These are a few near-at-hand samples of an evolution which is leaving some old occupations to history and scaring men with visions of starvation. Yet as one door is shut another and wider opens. There is always work enough for the earnest, the skilled, and the faithful. Labor leagues, which handicap the skilled and conscientious with the embarrassing weight of the unskilled, unconscientious, and dissipated, embarrass the situation, and time is needed to adjust the new conditions and correlations of the economic trend; but the law holds that *authentic progress creates more demand than it extinguishes.* Who sighs for a return to the sickle and hoe, the hand-rake and flail, the distaff and spinning-wheel, the ox-cart and stage-coach? If there are any outside the lunatic asylum who would annihilate the fruits of inventive genius and relegate to desuetude the splendid tokens of material advancement, let them speak, for them only have I offended.

FIFTH PAPER.

5. The *choice of occupations is voluntary, and regulated by adaptation, taste, occasion, and prospective profits.*

Progress and Poverty appears to assume that men are forced into uncomfortable and unprofitable employments by the fact that they have not access to land. As to this country, the assumption is gratuitous and grossly untrue. Our cities are thronged—I was near saying infested—with youths from country homes who seek more genteel and lucrative occupations than farming. The professions are crowded for similar reasons. It is purely a matter of choice. Not a few who are able to command means prefer to invest them in merchandise, manufactures, stocks, ships, or inventions, rather than in land. The slow gains and callous hands of tillage fail to captivate the youthful fancy; nor are city lots sure

enough of rapid appreciation to encourage outlay in that direction. Thousands in the southern counties of California are learning the
bitter lesson that land speculations and booms
are sometimes boomerangs. Many would
snatch eagerly at an opportunity to get back
half the cost of their bepraised acres.

Possibly a farmer may be found whose five
or more sons elect farming as their life-work ;
but such a case would be exceptional even in
the newer parts of the national domain. The
rule runs the other way.

6. *Dissipation, ignorance, poverty, and vice
are not effects of the private ownership of land.*
The opposite assumption, which runs through
and through *Progress and Poverty*, reverses the
verdict of history and audaciously belies candid
observation. The very reverse of the proposition is so nakedly true that one wonders at
the fatuity which dares to call it in question.

I mean to say that dissipation, voluntary
ignorance, idleness, and vice prevent men from
owning land or prospering in any thing. Look
in at the doors of saloons, visit the resorts of

Sabbath-breakers, count the hangers about in city and country-side, and see if you can make yourself believe that these loafers and bummers, these bloated and vicious, are all poor fellows who, but for the fact that Smith and Brown worked, saved, and bought land, would have been as wise as sages and as virtuous as saints ! The naked *petitio* of the book is entitled to notice only because of its earnest, endless, and audacious iteration.

If all the land were owned under the exclusive tax-scheme the idle could rent it in parcels and be much better off than the owners, for while, by Mr. George's plan, the full rental value would go to the State, the owner, besides getting nothing, would have the care and cost of repairs and general management.

It is not true that in this country there is a scarcity of land.

Improved hill farms in New Hampshire and Vermont are selling for a fraction of the cost of the improvements.

In 1886–88 the patents issued for government lands averaged thirty thousand a year.

In 1889 more than seventy thousand were issued, and the entries kept pace with the patents.

Up to last June one half of the two Dakotas was unentered.   In several other States settlements are outrunning government surveys.

In Idaho only about one seventh of the State is surveyed.

Vast tracts are being purchased from the Indians.

More than twenty million acres, forfeited by railroad corporations, are suspended, and only await congressional action to open them to settlement.

There are so-called desert lands, only needing practicable irrigation, enough in extent to support the entire present population of our country.

A large part of the land now under private ownership is not utilized, and a very small part of the cultivated tracts is brought up to its highest capacity.

In the Southern and South-western States are extensive and fertile areas held at low prices.

I confidently submit that such facts outweigh the too hasty generalizations of the esteemed author of *Progress and Poverty*. The resources of the United States and Territories are ample to feed, house, and clothe the entire present population of the planet, and all the·Old World countries have yet open space; and South America has immense stretches of fertile soil in its virgin state eagerly inviting landless millions to come and till and eat. Mexico, our next-door neighbor, is lonely for inhabitants and offers millions of acres for a bagatelle.

Mr. George's stand-point appears always to be within eye-shot of the landed estates of insular and continental Europe, which were never bought nor earned, but given by caprice to the tools and favorites of royalty and preserved intact by laws of primogeniture and entail. True, that which was wrong at the beginning cannot be made right by lapse of time. Yet his patent remedy, with its fatal self-negation, would afford no relief to the poor even there. In this country conditions are wholly different. Every acre has been bought of government, earned by reclamation and other improvements, or given in small tracts for military service. Large estates, with no laws of primogeniture and entail to preserve them, are broken up in the second and third generation. The sons of the rich become poor and the sons of the poor rich. The wheel of fortune is evermore carrying up and carrying down.

Even in the old and densely peopled divisions of the earth there is room. I borrow statistics from *Progress and Poverty*, sure that the author will not dispute his own figures. On page 101 we have these figures: "According to the estimates of MM. Behm and Wagner the population of India is but 132 to the square mile, and that of China 119, whereas Saxony has 442, England 422, the Netherlands 291, Italy 234, and Japan 233. There are thus in both countries [India and China] large areas unused or not fully used; but even in their more densely populated districts there can be no doubt that either could maintain a much greater population in a much higher degree of comfort, for in both countries is labor applied to production in the rudest and most inefficient way, and in both countries great natural resources are wholly neglected."

One of the large islands of Japan is very thinly inhabited. Africa, an old land, is still virgin and offers immense opportunities to enterprise and philanthropy. Stanley estimates that every one of the seven millions of our colored people could find a good-sized farm in the wide, rich, well-watered, salubrious wilderness which he traversed between the eastern borders of the Congo Free State and the Albert Nyanza. Frenchmen are now proving that even Sahara can be made to blossom as the rose.

Such facts as these, I again submit, ought to relieve any sense of suffocation we may have experienced from a fancied want of room. *Facts are stronger than fancies.*

SIXTH PAPER.

7. MR. GEORGE *makes no account of the vital bearing which different types of government must have on the practicability of such a scheme as he advocates.*

In a severe analysis there are but three kinds of government—namely, kinghood, priesthood, and manhood. All shapes and shades between are of the nature of varieties, not species. Each type grows from some germinant idea, some commanding seed-thought, and builds about the central principle institutions suited to its nature. Hence what is practicable under one form may prove wholly impracticable and disruptive under another.

The American government is of the manhood sort. It is " of the people, by the people, for the people." All legislation, all exhibitions of executive force, all armaments, are not for the prince or the priest, but for the man.

Hence the wide distribution of the suffrage, the freedom of press, pulpit, and forum, the common-school provision for universal education, the rule of majorities, and, in a word, the impressive and unquestioned recognition of a divine and universal endowment of " inalienable rights, among which are life, liberty, and the pursuit of happiness."

" The State is all of us." The fundamental government is all of us. Original power, under God, lodges with the people. Functional government, consisting of presidents, congresses, courts, constabulary, is a thing of convenience, a medium through which the fundamental government administers by the authority and will of the people. It can never rise above the source of its authority, nor for any considerable length of time sink below it. The technical government, therefore, in its structural plan and actual working, is a true index of the average intelligence and ethical stamina of the millions.

Under such a system there must exist great freedom of individual choice. Men choose

their callings, politics, and parties. They
cannot be assigned and classified, transferred
by sale or caprice of masterhood, located and
employed like serfs of the soil, or impressed
into service for wars of conquest, or shipped in
the national navy *nolens volens*. What, therefore, might be done in the way of raising discriminating taxes under a tyranny can never be
accomplished here without revolution, blood-
shed, and the annihilation of the freedom in
which we glory.

There are governmental methods so narrow,
so personal, so absolute in the power of life and
death, as to suggest the possibility of the con-
tinued and adequate cultivation of the soil under
the single-tax idea. Mr. George (pages 368,
369) states very mixedly and with capricious
application a sound principle of governmental
economy. Speaking of production, he says:
"This checking of production is, in a greater
or less degree, characteristic of most of the
taxes by which the revenues of modern govern-
ments are raised. All taxes upon manufactures,
all taxes upon commerce, all taxes upon capital,

all taxes upon improvements, are of this kind.
Their tendency is the same as that of Mo-
hammed Ali's tax on date-trees, though their
effect may not be so clearly seen. All such
taxes have a tendency to reduce production of
wealth, and should, therefore, never be resorted
to when it is possible to raise money by taxes
which do not check production."

More clearly stated and more justly applied,
the principle is this: Unequal and oppressive
taxation tends to diminish production, and,
especially with respect to useful and necessary
products, will never be resorted to by a wise
and just government.

Let us see how this principle applies to the
products which labor brings forth from the
soil. Here, again, I will consent to be indebted
to Mr. George for facts which refute his
favorite theory. Thus on pages 101–103 he
quotes with approval and comments with confidence as follows:

"In India from time immemorial the working classes have been ground down by exactions and oppressions into a condition of

hopeless and helpless degradation. For ages
and ages the cultivator of the soil has esteemed himself happy if, of his produce,
the extortion of the strong hand left him
enough to support life and furnish seed.
Capital could nowhere be safely accumulated
or to any considerable extent be used to assist
production. Is it not clear that this tyranny
and insecurity have produced the want and
starvation of India; and not, as according to
Buckle, the pressure of population upon sub-
sistence that has produced the want, and the
want the tyranny? Says the Rev. William
Tennant, a chaplain in the service of the East
India Company, writing in 1796, two years before the publication of the *Essay on Population :*
' When we reflect upon the great fertility of
Hindustan it is amazing to consider the fre-
quency of famine. It is evidently not owing
to any sterility of soil or climate; the evil
must be traced to some political cause, and it
requires but little penetration to discover it in
the avarice and extortion of the various gov-
ernments. The great spur to industry, that

VS. " PROGRESS AND POVERTY."   47

of security, is taken away. Hence no man raises more grain than is barely sufficient for himself, and the first unfavorable season produces famine. The Mogul government at no period offered full security to the prince, still less to his vassals, and to the peasants the most scanty protection of all. It was a continual tissue of violence and insurrection, treachery and punishment, under which neither commerce nor arts could prosper, nor agriculture assume the appearance of a system. . . . The rents to government were, and, where natives rule, still are, levied twice a year by a merciless banditti under the semblance of an army, who wantonly destroy or carry off whatever part of the produce may satisfy their caprice or satiate their avidity.' . . .

"To this merciless rapacity, which would have produced want and famine were the population but one to a square mile, and the land a garden of Eden, succeeded, in the first era of British rule in India, as merciless a rapacity backed by a far more irresistible power. . . .

"Upon horrors that Macaulay thus but

touches, the vivid eloquence of Burke throws a
stronger light : 'Whole districts surrendered to
the unrestrained cupidity of the worst of human
kind, poverty-stricken peasants fiendishly tort-
ured to compel them to give up their little
hoards, and once populous tracts turned into
deserts.' "

On page 105 Mr. George ingenuously adds :
" In other parts [of India], where the rent is
still taken by the State in the shape of a land-
tax, assessments are so high, and taxes are collected so relentlessly, as to drive the ryots
[farmers], who get but the most scanty living
in good seasons, into the claws of money-
lenders, who are, if possible, more rapacious
than the zemindars."

Again, pages 105, 106, Mr. George quotes
from Florence Nightingale : " The saddest
sight to be seen in the East—nay, probably in
the whole world—is the peasants of our Eastern empire." And Mr. George adds : " She
goes on to show the cause of the terrible fam-
ines, in taxation which takes from the culti-
vators the very means of cultivation, and the

actual slavery to which the ryots are reduced as
the consequence of our laws, producing in the
most fertile country in the world a grinding,
chronic semi-starvation in many places where
what is called famine does not exist."

Page 380, from Mrs. Fawcett: "In a great
part of India the land is owned by the government, and therefore the land-tax is rent paid
directly to the State. The economic perfection
of this system of tenure may be readily perceived." So we think! and the more clearly
perceived the more intensely abhorred.

Thus, in zealously attacking the theory of
Malthus, Mr. George lays a perilous stock
of dynamite underneath his own.

It would be easy to add Burma and Daho-
mey and parts of Russia to India to darken the
picture of oppression and desolation wrought
by exclusive and excessive land-tax, where
nothing less than the life-and-death power
of rulers could compel the crushed peasants to produce food enough for daily consumption. The noblest and fundamental
industry on which prosperity and life itself

4

depend is thus crippled, discouraged, and put to shame.

These gloomy pictures are but foreshadows of facts under which the tillers of our own soil would groan if power were given to the government to enforce the single-tax theory. Happily such a power does not exist; and therefore such a theory can never take effect till the freedom of our representative Republic gives place to hereditary monarchy or oligarchy clothed with the power of life and death. Until then the "peasants" of America will constitute a powerful part of the commonwealth of freedom, and will neither clamor for nor submit to unequal and unjust taxation. The waves of Boston Harbor still taste of tea.

SEVENTH PAPER.

MR. GEORGE proposes that land-owners shall not only be taxed to defray the entire running expenses of the government, but also to provide for immense outlays for improvements on a scale of grandeur heretofore unknown. Thus on page 365: "It will be necessary, where rent exceeds the present governmental revenues, to commensurately increase the amount demanded in taxation, and to continue this increase as society progresses and rent advances."

Again, page 410: "There would be a great and increasing surplus revenue from the taxation of land values; for material progress, which would go on with greatly accelerated rapidity, would tend constantly to increase rent. This revenue arising from the common property could be applied to the common benefit, as were the revenues of Sparta. We might not establish public tables—they would be unnecessary; but we would establish public baths, museums, libraries, gardens, lecture-rooms, music and dancing halls, theaters, universities, technical schools, shooting-galleries, playgrounds, gymnasiums, etc. Heat, light, and motive-power, as well as water, might be conducted through our streets at public expense; our roads be lined with fruit-trees; discoverers and inventors rewarded; scientific investigations supported, and in a thousand ways the public revenues made to foster efforts for the public benefit."

There you have it in a nutshell. All capital, commerce, banks, mills, manufactories, ships, railroads, left untaxed. The vast majority left scot-free of taxation and munificently supplied with luxuries, all at the expense of the land-owners, a minority, and, taken as a whole, the hardest worked and poorest paid and least benefited class in the body politic. If that is justice give us tyranny. The vast body of land sold by the State is owned by small farmers, who are under such pressure that Senator Stanford is now pressing upon

Congress a measure of relief in the form of a bill authorizing the government to loan them money at two per cent., to release them from the grasp of the Shylock capitalists whom Mr. George would tenderly release from the burden of taxation.

Mr. George will find it easy to remind us that the American government is not like the misgovernments we were dwelling upon a little ago, but hard enough to convince a thinker that the difference is not fatally against the practicability of his theory. American farmers are not like the fellahs of Egypt, the serfs of Russia, and the ryots of India. Nothing less than a regression, intellectual, moral, governmental, to the condition of power and slavery prevalent in India under the rajahs, and Burma under her merciless kings, could make possible, on our soil, a policy of discriminative injustice and class helotage long since outgrown by most civilized and by all Christian nations.

8. *There is a marked peculiarity in our author's habit of thought.* It is what the Ger-

mans call an intense mind. Collaterals and sequences have no weight. Having espoused a theory, every thing must give it right of way. It becomes a sort of double-ender which runs one way as well as another. This idiosyncrasy crops out again and again. As a sample see page 100. The theory of Malthus is under fierce attack. Mr. George must prove that increase of population does not diminish the relative supply of sustenance, and this is one of the ways he does it: " Increase of descendants does not show increase of population. It could only do this when the breeding was in and in. Smith and his wife have a son and daughter, who marry some one else's daughter and son, and each have two children. Smith and his wife would thus have four grandchildren, but there would be in the one generation no greater number than in the other—each child would have four grandparents. And, supposing this process to go on, the line of descent might constantly spread out into hundreds, thousands, millions, but in each generation of descendants there would be no more individuals than in any previous generation of ancestors."

The hypothesis—without stopping to inquire about its pertinence—is novel and astounding. If it is luminous to the reader I congratulate him. Is there a law limiting the propagation of the species to this two-and-two arrangement? Suppose Smith's son and daughter should have ten children each, how would the figures stand? Henry Ward Beecher said it interested him less to learn whether he descended from an ape than to know how far he had got from the ancestral starting-point. The puzzle with me is to divine, on such a genealogical basis, how we ever got so far from Adam, and especially how there came to be so many Smiths in the world.

The same habitude carries itself into a variety of cases. Collaterals are ignored, and the good of whatever the author opposes is to him an unknown quantity. He thinks he sees clearly that land bought with capital should be taxed, but capital derived from land should be exempt; that bonds or greenbacks loaned on interest should be exempt, but land bought with bonds or greenbacks should be taxed to the full amount of the rent it will bring; that tenement-houses, crops, banks, mills, should be exempt, but the land on which the crops and timber grew and the stone was quarried and the iron mined should bear all the burdens of government; that a paralytic or a widow who owns a little farm, the rent of which is his or her only support, should turn all that rent into the public treasury to pay for governmental protection of palaces of luxury, marts of business, public baths, theaters, playgrounds, dance-halls, for landless millionaires and loafing tramps, mechanics, merchants, and dudes, on whom no burden, not even a head-tax, is to be laid.

EIGHTH PAPER.

A SIMILAR ophthalmia shows itself in much
that is said about corporations, monopolies,
and protective duties.   On pages 369, 370 we
learn that " there are also the onerous monopolies alluded to in Chapter IV of Book III,
which result from the aggregation of capital in
businesses which are of the nature of monopolies.   But while it would be extremely diffi-
cult, if not altogether impossible, to lay taxes
by general law so that they would fall exclu-
sively on the returns of such monopoly, and
not become taxes on production and exchange,
it is much better that these monopolies should
be abolished.   The reason that residents of
Nevada are compelled to pay as much freight
from the East as though their goods were
carried to San Francisco and back again is
that the authority which prevents extortion
on the part of a hack-driver is not exercised in

respect to a railroad company. It may be said generally that businesses which are in their nature monopolies are properly part of the function of the State."

Again, with respect to the privileges granted to corporations, Mr. George says on pages 173, 174: "It is a power of the same kind as that which James granted to Buckingham, and it is often exercised with as reckless a disregard, not only of the industrial, but of the personal, rights of individuals. A railroad approaches a small town as a highwayman approaches his victim. The threat that 'if you do not accede to our terms we will leave your town two or three miles to one side' is as efficacious as a 'stand and deliver,' when the threat of the railroad company is not merely to deprive the town of the benefits which the railroad might give; it is to put it in a far worse position than if no railroad had been built. . . . And just as robbers unite to plunder in concert and divide the spoil, so do the trunk lines of railroads unite to raise rates and pool their earnings, or the Pacific roads form a combination with the Pacific Mail

Steamship Company by which toll-gates are virtually established on land and ocean. And just as Buckingham's creatures, under authority of the gold-thread patent, searched private houses and seized papers and persons for purposes of lust and extortion, so does the great telegraph company, which, by the power of associated capital, deprives the people of the United States of the full benefit of a beneficent invention, tamper with correspondence and crush out newspapers which offend it." Yet this oppressive associated capital must remain forever untaxed!

Mr. George is as much displeased with customs and protection as with railroad and steamship corporations. Strangely enough, he seems to see that the farmer class, on whom and other land-owners he proposes to lay the entire pecuniary burdens of government, are cruelly wronged by the encouragement given to home manufactures by protection.

To all this it is just to answer:

1. Great enterprises demand co-operation of forces and combinations of capital. These

are the "power," and all that is asked of government is liberty to exercise the power on some portion of the public domain. Such liberty granted to corporations does not constitute them monopolies, unless others are "prohibited under severe penalties," as in the case of Buckingham's gold-thread monopoly, from forming similar combinations for similar purposes. The rights granted to corporations by our government do not include such restrictions. A railroad, therefore, is no more a monopoly than a turnpike. Government, in any and every case, has power to fix the rate of toll, the price of donated land, etc. On a smaller scale, but on the same underlying principle, the first blacksmith's shop or grist-mill is a monopoly, by consequence of being first in the field.

2. These improved mediums of transportation and commerce leave the old ways open to all who prefer them. The impatient and complaining are free to ship their goods around the Horn, cross the plains on muleback, and send their messages by mail as aforetime.

3. The "robbery" of towns is not always a stand-and-deliver process. More than once I have known small towns to refuse or charge exorbitantly for right of way, and then curse the corporation roundly for running by on the outside. As to freight charges, they are some-times regulated by the labor and expense of discharging. A man in Nevada, for instance, sends East for a barrel of oatmeal from Akron, a box of soap from Chicago, and a bundle of buggy-spokes from Omaha, and can see no rea-son why a train cannot stop in front of his little way-side store, overhandle two or three car-loads of freight and leave his packages, and raves because they are carried on to the ter-minus and sent back by return train with full charges. There may have been real instances of carelessness and injustice ; but many assumed causes of complaint are unthoughtful and pee-vish. The old ways are open to the complain-ant in every case.

4. Rates of passage. It cost me four hun-dred and twenty-five dollars and twenty-seven days of seasickness to come to California. Yet

I accounted the Isthmus a great improvement
on the Cape Horn route and the plains. Now
we cross the plains in five days in an elegant
drawing-room on wheels, at a cost of a hundred or so dollars. That I must pronounce a
still greater gain to both comfort and purse.
If any prefer the earlier way, it is a free
country.

5. I wish to communicate with New York
in an emergency. Valuable interests are at
stake. The mail will carry my message in a
week, the telegraph will send it in five minutes.
There is a gain of eighty-six hundred and thirty-
five minutes. It is optional with me to use the
one or the other.

"But," it is urged, "the government ought
to own all these things, and then—" Then
what? Would trains and steamships and telegraph run by magic if the government owned
them? Comparison shows that governmental
management is more expensive than private,
as a rule, the world over. Then, too, there
would be no competition and no stimulus to
private enterprise to expedite business and

reduce rates. No short roads would be run for convenience of localities, and endless local jealousies would attend every line of national improvement.

"But do you not see that land-owners are to furnish funds for all these public conveniences?" So, so. And then the landless and the lazy may ride, roll, travel, dispatch, dance, and bathe twelve hours a day, and not a dime to pay! Will not that be glorious?

6. It usually happens that private enterprise outruns official tardiness and red tape—as in the case of the corporations denounced by Mr. George—much to the advantage of the commonwealth. Take the Union and Central Pacific roads, constituting our transcontinental line, as a sample, and reflect upon the circumstances under which it was built. It appeared likely to prove a vital condition of national self-protection. Indeed, it might prove so in any crisis. But the government was not in a spirit to inaugurate or a condition to prosecute such a work, neither is there a shadow of probability that it would have been as quickly or inexpen-

sively done, if done at all.   It was undertaken at great risk to its projectors, and prosecuted with an energy scarcely paralleled in history. Its projectors were not men of large wealth, but of far-sightedness and indomitable courage.   It was to traverse wide unsettled regions which had no appreciable value and could yield no commerce except as the road might create it, and was to surmount mountain chains which would have terrified more timid natures.   They risked every thing, even life itself—as in a notable instance in the career of Charles Crocker —to do a work which assured and enriched the nation far beyond its cost.   Yet that it was not and is not a monopoly is demonstrated by the fact that competing lines already stretch from ocean to ocean.

NINTH PAPER.

7. THE field was an open one. Mr. George and I had as much right to build a road as Stanford, Crocker, Huntington, and Hopkins. And we had nearly as much money, for all they had was a bagatelle compared with the expense to be incurred. What we lacked was foresight, faith, courage, and possibly clear-sighted patriotism. It does not impress me as generous or just to denounce them because they outsaw and outgeneraled us. Courage and faith were needed. I well remember when groups of men used to stand on the streets in Sacramento and laugh loud and long at " the blamed fools who thought they were going to run a railroad over the tops of the Sierra Nevada Mountains."

8. In a word, whatever evitable or inevitable injury it may have wrought in exceptional cases, it is only just to concede that the bene-

5

fits to the State by the railroad a thousand times outweigh the real or imaginary harm. And it is to be regretted that the loose and reasonless clamor raised by pessimists and demagogues, and echoed by the thriftless and shallow-thinking, should be emboldened by the one-sided and *ex cathedra* pronouncements of so able and influential a man as the author of *Progress and Poverty*. Would the country or one man in it be better off if the road had not been built? Take a case as a sample of the prevalent ructation, and also of the injury done to farmers by the road. In one of our large valleys a not over thrifty farmer was cursing the railroad corporation as a grinding monopoly. A by-stander said:

" I would not live under such tyranny. Sell out and leave. What will you take for your farm?"

He must have thirty-five dollars an acre if he sold, but he didn't care to sell.

" What was your land worth before the railroad came?"

" Wal, about five dollars."

" That is one way the cruel road has crushed you. Now, what else has it done? The guilty wretches of this heartless corporation have killed your mules, haven't they?"

Why, no, they hadn't.

" Well, they have burned your wagons?"

No, of course they hadn't.

"Surely, now, they have torn up and destroyed all your wagon roads?"

Pshaw, no, they hadn't done any such thing.

" Then I'll tell you what to do. Just load your grain into your wagons and haul it to market as you used to. And when you wish to go to San Francisco saddle your horse—don't count the horse or your own time any thing—make the trip in five days, and pay about three times as much as it costs you now to get into a car at eleven o'clock P. M., go to the city, transact your business, and get home for tea next day, with lodging included in your fare. True, it will not be nearly as cheap, comfortable, and expeditious, but you will show that you are a free American citizen and don't propose to be crushed by the iron heel of a soulless monopoly."

The man looked foolish, but I presume he is still denouncing the wicked corporation as often as any are lazy or sympathetic enough to stop to listen.

9. Mr. George's resentment against the policy of protection is as pronounced as against railroads. He thinks he sees how small farmers especially are robbed by the tariff which encourages home manufacture.

Many thoughtful persons judge differently. As a class small farmers are small purchasers of foreign goods. It appears to many men of sound mind that a hungry home market is most stable and most profitable. It is certainly most convenient. Such a market results from a balancing of industries under which manufactories hold their place and rightful share in the prevalent industrial economy, thus bringing demand door to door with supply. Many wise men think that national independence and readiness for emergencies depend on national sufficiency of indigenous resources, and that general thrift and prosperity result from the harmony and interplay thus encouraged.

One who studies the destitution of the South during the great civil war—a destitution attributable to the lack of manufactories—will learn a lesson from facts worth a thousand theories.   Possibly the devotees of free trade may think, like Stephenson about the cow, that if facts stand in the way of their favorite theory it will be so much the worse for the facts ; but it will not harm any of us to treat respectfully the holders of opposite opinions.

TENTH PAPER.

"PROGRESS AND POVERTY" *ignores, or but faintly hints at, the only remedy which can harmonize distribution with want and sweep the earth clear of injustice, greed, oppression, neglect, and hunger.*

To dream that certain legislative and economic adjustments would rid the race of its woes is but to dream. Such a fancy discredits history and covers human nature with obliviousness. Common ownership of land has been tried and found wanting. It was tried in Plymouth and failed. It was tried in Virginia and failed. It was tried at New Harmony and failed. It was tried at Mixville, N. Y., and failed. It was tried at Brook Farm, under the gifted Fourier, and failed. It is being tried in the poor, dry-rot colony of Acraria and is a failure. It has failed every-where. They soon discovered that, as in Virginia, many " worked

lazily and ate industriously." Private ownership was and is the lesson and the remedy
commended by experience.

A handful of Shakers, as at Harrodsburg,
Ky., holds itself together by religious bonds
and numerical insignificance, but the Friend
Quakers, for whom I ought to cherish a filial
reverence, are compelled to adhere to individual ownership. Just now a commanding conviction engages the public mind that land in
severalty—that is, private ownership—for the
Indians on reservations would be a marked improvement on the present policy. Such an
arrangement accords with sound philosophy
and the lessons of a world-wide experience.

To put land, mines, railroads, telegraphs, under control of government would be a freak of
madness. What *is* our government? There
are four words which Mr. George has a habit
of using interchangeably. They are We, State,
Government, Community. "We" have a right
to take all; the "State" has a right to take
all; the "Government" has a right to take
all; the "Community" has a right to take all.

Things equal to the same thing are equal to one another. But what is this multinomen, functionally considered? It is Smith, Brown, Jones, O'Reilly, and Spookenstaver, who have managed to get themselves elected to legislative, judicial, and executive offices for a term. That election does not confer infallibility is sadly demonstrated by the laws which they make, amend, repeal, break, contradictorily interpret, and capriciously enforce. Could a body of men capable of repealing the Sunday laws—the laborer's only legal defense against the exactions of greed and the oppressions of power—for the votes of the slums and the prurience of partisan victory ; or such a legislature as our last in California, which appeared to act the role of the false watchman within opening the door for bigger thieves without to reach the public treasury—could such a body, I say, be intrusted with the immense power and patronage for which Mr. George contends.

Doubtless many civil officers are able and upright, but the mixture, the changeableness, the partisan heat, and the irrepressible uncertainty of politics are too great to leave room for so egregious a confidence.

To seek intelligently for a cure we must first know the cause of the disease.   To ascribe vice, poverty, degradation, and crime to private ownership of land, we have seen, and may every-where see, is naked and ludicrous assumption.   In the same social grade, the same trade, the same place of residence, the same environments, there are always found instances of thrift and comfort side by side with squalor, filth, and wretchedness.   Even in London, where poverty and vice are supposed to seethe and swelter as almost nowhere else, the rule holds that " every man is the architect of his own fortune."   I quote from one who knows as well as any living man whereof he writes:

" I would not say hard words against poverty; wherever it comes it is bitter to all ; but you will mark, as you notice carefully, that a few are poor because of unavoidable circumstances. A very large share of the poverty of London is the sheer and clear result of profuseness, want of forethought, idleness, and, worst of all, drunkenness. Ah, that drunkenness! that is the master-evil. If drink could be got rid of we might be sure of conquering the devil himself. The drunkenness created by the infernal liquor-dens which plague-spot the whole of this huge city is appalling. No; I did not speak in haste or let slip a hasty word. Many of the drink-houses are nothing less than infernal. In some respects they are even worse, for hell has its use as a divine protest against sin ; but as for the gin-palace, there is nothing to be said in its favor. The vices of the age cause three fourths of its poverty. If you could look at the houses to-night, the wretched homes where women will tremble at the sound of their husband's foot as he comes home, where little children will crouch down with fear upon their little beds of straw, because the human brute who calls himself 'a man' will come reeling home from the palace where he has been indulging his appetite—if you could look at such a sight, and remember it will be seen ten thousand times over to-night, I think you would say, ' God help us by all

means to save some ! ' Since the great ax to lay
at the foot of this deadly upas-tree is the Gos-
pel of Christ, may God help us to hold that
ax there, and to work constantly with it, till
the huge trunk of the poison-tree begins to
rock to and fro, and we get it down, and London is saved from wretchedness and misery
which now drip from every bough."

The fact that one man owns land does not
make another man drunken and devilish. Mr.
George's sovereign " remedy " is about as
pertinent as the sum of a budding genius in
the district school : " If a peck of 'beans cost
nine pence, how far is it around a tremendously
big brush-heap ? " If " the vices of the age
cause three fourths of the poverty " (and that
estimate is below the mark), strike at the
vices—drunkenness, gambling, the house of
the strange woman, " whose steps take hold
on hell."

We punish a man for being drunk. Punish the men who make him drunk as well. We
inflict heavy penalties upon one who burns
houses, sells tainted meat or impure milk, then

license another to poison and despoil and turn
the homes of his patrons into hell-prisons where
the demonized "master " is police, judge, jury,
jailer, and executioner.   And Mr. George proposes to cure all this infernal array of deadly
blunders and dire distress with the single tax!

Inconsequently enough, the able author of
Progress and Poverty constructs of the evasions,
concealments, and outright lying of possessors
of other kinds of wealth an argument for laying
the whole burden of government upon land-
owners.   Thus on pages 374, 375: " The gross
corruptions and fraud occasioned in the United
States by the whisky and tobacco taxes are
well known ; the constant undervaluations of
the custom-house, the ridiculous untruthful-
ness of income-tax returns, and the absolute
impossibility of getting any thing like a just
valuation of personal property are matters of
notoriety. . . . Taxes which lack the item of
certainty tell most fearfully upon morals. Our
revenue laws as a body might well be entitled,
' Acts to promote the corruption of public
officials, to suppress honesty and encourage

fraud, to set a premium upon perjury and the subornation of perjury, and to divorce the idea of law from the idea of justice.' . . . The tax on land values, which is the least arbitrary of taxes, possesses in the highest degree the element of certainty. It may be assessed and collected with a definiteness that partakes of the immovable and unconcealable character of the land itself. Taxes levied on land may be collected to the last cent."

All which amounts to this : Five men are individually in my debt. One has bonds, one greenbacks, one a valuable patent-right, a fourth a clipper-ship, and the fifth a farm. The first conceals his bonds, the second belies his greenbacks, the third's patent is unattachable, the fourth sends his ship to Europe, the fifth— unlucky fellow!—cannot pocket his farm or falsify the county records; so I demand that he shall pay his own debt and the debts of the four rascals who are cheating me out of my honest dues.

One to five may not exactly state the relative number of land-owners as compared with non-owners, but exactness is not necessary to the point of the hypothesis. France has eight millions, which I infer includes only actual tillers of their own acres. These agriculturists and horticulturists are the keystone of the economic arch, the spinal column of the nation's patriotic strength. It is true of every country that the people attached to the soil by actual ownership have the most stable patriotism. Our population is flowing disproportionately into the cities. Probably the incoming census returns will show actual farmers in less proportion than in France, for the reason that machinery is more used here than there to augment the productiveness of labor. Does any man imagine that the eight millions, with the added owners of city lots in France, could be compelled, without bloody revolution, to defray all the current expenses of the State and provide luxuries for the millions of non-holding people? Yet it would be far easier to reach such a result there than here.

ELEVENTH PAPER.

Profit-sharing is a beneficent expedient which philanthropic individuals here and there are trying with success. Since 1878 a number of firms have adopted it as a stroke at once of policy and of justice ; among them the Pillsbury flour-mills of Minneapolis, Wanamaker in Philadelphia, the *Century Magazine*, the *Staats-Zeitung*, the Deering manufactory of agricultural implements in Chicago, Lewis Miller & Co., of Akron and Canton, O., and Proctor & Gamble in Cincinnati.

For more than thirty years a few houses in France, Sweden, and Germany have practiced this method with much satisfaction to all parties concerned. But profit-sharing must be left to individual impulse and honor. It cannot be governmentally instituted or enforced. The general adoption of such a scheme can be brought about only by some power that shall profoundly influence individual life and character.

It must needs be such a power as changed the imperious persecutor, Saul of Tarsus, into a fervent, tireless, self-forgetting toiler for the uplifting of the helpless, the hopeless, the heathen; such a power as placed John Newton, the slave-merchant—" the man-stealer," as he used to call himself—among the sleepless haters of all oppression; such a power as begot in the hearts of the cannibals of Fiji a sympathy so tender and a benevolence so uncalculating that nowhere in all the world are shipwrecked sailors more bravely rescued or kindly treated than on their coral-bound coasts; a power such as transformed bloody John Adams and his fellow-mutineers of the *Bounty*, with the wild women they picked up on the islands, into a model community, orderly, chaste, unselfish, morally heroic, till Pitcairn became one of the ethical light-houses of the ocean.

If similar evolutions could every-where prevail every man would be every man's brother.

The astute would befriend the dull, the strong
the weak, the learned the illiterate, the well
the sick, the rich the poor, as no legislation or
tax scheme could ever make them do. Help
would be instant, hearty, ample. To make
such a condition actual the millions must be
brought up to the experience which the ten thousands have exhibited. Enough have appeared,
as samples, amply to prove the attainableness
of so beneficent a spirit, so that the possibility
has passed beyond debate. It is a postulate
that the power which made new men of Saul,
Newton, Michael Varyana, and King Tom is
adequate to universal efficiency, if it could be
brought to bear.

It is both history and philosophy that the
ethical and spiritual forces which lift men the-
oretically and by conviction out of the deep
grooves of selfishness must arise from some
underlying religious faith. This ought not to
appear anomalous, for every civilization within
the reach of historic, traditional, and anti-
quarian research has rested on a substructure
of religion from which the moral element in
6

its laws, sentiments, and customs flowed. The character of the civilization has been determined by the quality of the religious basis. Hence a weak religious system has sustained a dubious and unprogressive civilization ; and whenever the progress of a people has exhausted the ethical upflow stagnation or retrogression has followed. This has been true of the old pagan civilizations for a thousand years. A limitlessly progressive civilization must be nourished by an undergirding religion whose ethical supply can never be exhausted.

But one such religion is known. But one such is needed. The ripest fruit of the old book religions is " the golden rule of Confucius," which is negative, timid, selfish, and provides only for the do-nothing side of our life. A man may be the veriest churl, shutting himself within himself, never doing a noble or humane deed from the cradle to the coffin, and keep the Confucian rule. The positive doing side it leaves wholly unfurnished.

An economy of instruction and uplifting sufficient to harmonize liberality with need on a

universal scale must embrace these four partic-
ulars :

1. A correct theory of life.

2. An adequate motive power.

3. A reconstructive or regenerative power
strong enough to overcome natural inertia and
self-seeking.

4. The economy of life and provision of
power must be clearly set forth in available
form and diligently propagated by the recip-
ients of the resulting benefit.

I. *There is such a theory of life.*

John Adams and the mutineers learned. it
from an old book picked out of a seaman's
chest. The Fijians read it in the same book.
Thousands of thousands have gleaned the
lesson from the same source. To that book
we shall do well that we take heed as unto a
light that shineth in a dark place. It is not
the Shastras, the Zend Avesta, *The Book of
Mormon*, nor *The Light of Asia*. The book
to which I allude is as perfectly suited to this
age as though intended for no other, and to
every man as thought studiously written for

him alone.   The sage and the savage, the Ka-
fir and the Hottentot, the Bushman and the
" red-browed forest ranger," all find in this one
volume perfect portraitures, profound needs,
and adequate supplies.

*Here are samples of the practical lessons of
the book*—a few of its broad rules of life: The
end of the commandment is love.   Let love
be without dissimulation.   Love is the fulfilling of the law.   Love worketh no ill to his
neighbor, therefore it is the fulfilling of the law.
Deal thy bread to the hungry, and bring the
poor that are cast out to thy house.   Visit the
widow and fatherless in their affliction.   Devise
not evil against thy neighbor, nor take up a
reproach against him.   That which is altogether just shalt thou do.   Thou shalt not de-
fraud thy neighbor.   The wages of him that is
hired shall not abide with thee all night until
the morning.   Do good to them that hate you.
If thine enemy hunger, feed him.   If there be
any other commandment it is briefly comprehended in this, namely, Thou shalt love thy
neighbor as thyself.   Whatsoever ye would

that men should do to you, do ye even so to them.

II. *There is no adequate motivity.*

1. *The doctrine of immortality.* We shall meet again and remember. When James C. Jones, the most accomplished governor that ever honored Tennessee (and that is saying much) went down from the little farm to Pulaski in butternut-colored jeans some sons of rich men sneered and pointed fingers. They met him again when he held listening thousands captivated, spell-bound by his wonderful eloquence; and while rich and poor pressed forward for the honor of taking his hand the poor creatures remembered and slunk away. There is mighty inspiration to good and mighty restraint of evil in a belief in immortality. A distinguished editor of a secular journal, still throned on the tripod, said to the students of our university, "You might as well attempt to make a passion-flower out of a cabbage-stalk as any thing grand and noble out of men who have no faith in a future life."

2. *Brotherhood is another element in the tre-mendous motive force.* It is the special plead-ing of prejudice, and not the dictum of a broad and ripe anthropology, which denies that "God hath made of one blood all nations of men for to dwell on all the face of the earth." "Love as brethren, be pitiful, be courteous." "Whoso hath this world's good, and seeth his brother have need, and shutteth up his bowels of compassion from him, how dwelleth the love of God in him?" "Whosoever hateth his brother is a murderer." Such are a few of the fair inferences and incentives drawn from brotherhood.

3. *Gratitude and example.* One of the world's heroes, whose grand life and superb powers were consecrated to the purest philanthropy, who sacrificed fame and riches, and endured hunger, stripes, shipwrecks, dungeons, and death for the Master whom he served, left on record this sufficient explanation: "The love of Christ constraineth us; because we thus judge, that if one died for all, then were all dead: and that he died for all, that they which

live should not henceforth live unto themselves, but unto him which died for them, and
rose again." The inference is full of pathos
and power: "If he laid down his life for us,
we ought to be willing to lay down our lives
for the brethren." Gratitude is the noblest in-
gredient in rational happiness, and the strongest incentive to benevolent activity. Let the
truth get commanding possession of any man
that One bore his sicknesses and carried his
sorrows, was bruised for his iniquities and
wounded for his transgressions, chastised for
his peace and crucified for his redemption,
and let him realize that this glorious Being
wishes him for his sake to feed the hungry,
comfort the sorrowing, shield the endangered,
and rescue the lost, and every energy of life
will be set in motion. Labor will no longer
prove a load nor duty seem a task.

4. *Rewards.* The All-Father treats us according to the laws of our nature. If he calls
us to a mission of sacrifice he holds before us
a "recompense of reward," under the incite-
ment of which a young man of rarest gifts,

the greatest statesman of the race, adopted
into royal heirship and in sight of a throne,
turned from crown and scepter to associate
with slaves and lead a thankless people through
weary years of desert life, die alone, and sleep
in an unmonumented grave. Here is the solv-
ent of the mystery of consecrated lives. Here
is the exegesis of the lesson: " He that loveth
not his brother whom he hath seen, how can
he love God whom he hath not seen?"   Here
we recognize the obeyableness of the command that "he that loveth God love his
brother also."

The reward is gracious, not equivalent;
a divinely royal bounty, not an arithmetical
price. The order of the government is this:
To them who by patient continuance in well-
doing seek for glory, honor, and incorruption,
God will recompense eternal life.

TWELFTH PAPER.

III. There *is regenerative power to harmon-ize mind and heart with rule and motive.*

It is not our own will, though that must be consenting.   It is not self-discipline, though that has its uses.   It is not the help of men or angels, though sympathy, human or angelic, is grateful.   It is not psychical, for the intellect may be intensely alive and the ideality per-fect, yet the man remain selfish, sordid, sensual, devilish, spiritually dead.

He only who fashioned the eye can fathom the mysteries of life and lift lapsed humanity out of derangement and diseased proclivity into a new life, the broken spring mended, the lost balance restored, and a new law written in the members.

That a transforming power exists is placed beyond dispute by numberless instances of its wonder-working.   It lifts the fierce into gentleness, the arrogant into meekness, the proud into humility, the self-seeking into self-forgetfulness. It has achieved this change among men of all tongues, ranks, colors, ages. It has wrought the change among thousands of thousands; it is doing it among thousands of thousands now. I am not now asking you to concede the divineness of the record, but you will have to admit the force of facts. Peace has come to disordered homes and love-rest to troubled hearts through this power. Reason about it as we will, its nature, origin, *modus*, it is self-proved, witnessed by unimpeachable and overwhelming testimony. It is too obvious for argument that the Power which molded the fierce Fijian man-eater into a meek preacher of righteousness, set King Tom in calm and fearless opposition to the fetichism and all the abominations of his own and surrounding tribes, and transformed the bloody Tsimshean Indians into an industrious and loving Christian community now at Metlahkahtla is able to "make the Ethiop white."

A full revelation of this grand scheme of reform is found in one book only. Christmas Evans found it there, and there the Fingo finds it—a book which promotes every possible virtue and discourages every possible vice. Unlike the thirty yards of the books of Buddhism, this volume teaches by principles as broad as the domain of human life and plain enough to be understood by wayfaring men. It is a book that invites criticism and challenges competition; that furnishes every man in every emergency with the wisest of lessons and the most wholesome of motives, and is perfectly fitted to the needs of every stage of civilization. Concerning this volume Sir Walter Scott said, " There is but one book." Happy the homes in which its lessons are devoutly studied! Happy the country in whose schools and courts it is recognized as the one authority in morals !

GENERAL RESULTS.

I RESPECTFULLY submit that we have fairly reached the following conclusions :

1. That Mr. George's patent definitions do not in any degree modify the actual issues of things, nor in any measure support his high single-tax theory.

2. That the distinction he makes as to rightfulness of ownership, between the products of labor expended on land and that expended otherwise, indicates imperfect knowledge and leads to crude generalizations.

3. That the assumption that private ownership of land is the cause of the ignorance, poverty, degradation, and vice which we deplore is too false to be presented as fact and too thin to be offered as hypothesis.

4. That a functional government, ruled by ballots and administered by political parties, would be rent asunder by an attempt to inaugurate the single-tax scheme.

5. That the government would be slower and less distributive and more expensive than private enterprise in building improvements.

6. That political revolutions and provincial jealousies would be created by every attempt of the government to improve one section rather than another.

7. That in attempting to avoid the " shock " liable to attend his scheme of reform by conceding perpetual retention and management, with power to sell, will, rent, and devise unlimited bodies of land now in possession or yet to be possessed, Mr. George takes the spinal marrow out of his whole scheme and greatly aggravates any evils which are liable to lead to the oppression of the hireling in his wages.

8. That his " True Remedy," the single tax, is retrogressive, unstatesmanlike, unjust, impolitic, one-eyed, impudent, outrageous, and can never be carried into effect among a free and self-respecting people. The fundamental industry which feeds the nation and makes all other industries possible, will never submit to

the enormous and insane proposition until the forms and the very name of free government are obsolescent and the spirit of liberty expires.

9. As I see it, no self-respecting American citizen capable of comprehending relations and foreseeing consequences will for a moment tolerate the thought of desiring, or will consent to receive, his safety and sustenance at the expense of others. Every honest man prefers to pay his own bills. The good God grant that the spirit of robbery and mendicity may always be foreign on American soil!

10. Authentic Christianity, as a social and experimental force, will yield all that is beneficent in economics, all that is loyal in citizenship, all that is faithful in domestic relations, all that is just in business, all that is liberal in benevolence, all that is generous in sentiment, all that is magnanimous in judgment, all that is brave in righteousness, all that is noble in manhood. It is therefore the ONE REMEDY for which piety should pray and patriotism labor, and courage dare, and

zeal proclaim, and faith "lend its realizing light." But it must be the genuine article. No sham, no counterfeit, no make-believe, no necromantic pudding of admixture will serve. Veritable Christliness perfectly answers to the high demand. It will solve the labor problem, purge social impurity, cure laziness, quench greed, and give to every man who opens wide his heart and understanding to its sway a brother's hand of help. Until then—until law enters into life—life will evade law.

11. Therefore, missing, as it does, philosophy, justice, and regenerative power; ignoring, as it does, the lessons of history and vast experience; ignoring, as it does, the forecasting of consequences; assuming, as it does, what it was impossible to prove; and arguing, as it does, on false and impertinent premises; encouraging, as it does, irrational and falsely explained discontent; stimulating, as it does, class hatred and feculent thoughts of confiscation and spoliation; and striking, as it does, at the fundamental industry which is the taproot of national prosperity, the scheme of

Progress   and   Poverty should henceforth wear
the truer label, REGRESS AND SLAVERY.

UNDERGIRDING principles of well-ordered
life which are contravened, infracted, or ignored by the single-tax *theory :*

1. The free play of individuality, under the
stimulus of personal accountability and the
restraints of justice and the claims of brotherhood, is essential to the highest type of civilization and the most exalted and efficacious
development of religion.

2. Agriculture is the fundamental industry
on which all prosperity rests, and the ownership
in fee simple of a home is promotive of the
home-loves and homely virtues which are vital
to patriotism.   Any policy which tends to
degrade the one and discourage the other is
detrimental and dangerous in proportion to the
measure of its popular acceptance.

3. Any plan of government and law which
promises the lazy, the selfish, the unthrifty, and
the unjust an exceptional class to bear the
financial burdens of civilization for them is a

deep and demoralizing injury to the disbur-
dened and a cruel injustice to the overburdened.

4. Any scheme which ignores the inborn
selfishness of human nature and builds its
Utopia of universal happiness upon political
adjustments and human law, ignoring the
heart-renewing power of God and the Christ-
born heart-love for Jew and Samaritan, Par-
thian and Mede, Elamite and Cappadocian, is
a dream as idle and childish as the vagaries of
madmen or the drivel of idiots.

5. Any proposal of reform which attributes
the poverty and discontent of the dissipated
and unthrifty to other than their true causes is
an aggravation of the evil by the false methods
of the attempted cure.   It is poison and pesti-
lence in the social atmosphere.

6. Any doctrine which encourages men to
curse their " misfortune " and dream covetously
of unearned riches, instead of " working with
their hands [and heads] the thing that is
good," is a mischievous fallacy and a political
endangerment.

7. The notion that the only " laboring

7

classes" are hand-workers, and that riches accumulated by righteous enterprise in developing virgin resources are an injury to the "toiling masses," is fit only for the distempered brain of a paralogist.

8. The fancy that if the "government" owned all lines of public conveyance it could run them cheaper, pay better wages, and incur less risk of malfeasance and mismanagement than competing private corporations is a speculation which flies in the face of rational probability and the suggestions of experience. Even now the clamor for an eight-hour law and exceptional wages for all public employment has more weight with "government" and the average politician than the sweating brows and calloused hands of the uncomplaining whose toil, in field and shop and ship and office, must pay the unjust and discriminating score.

9. Any policy of government which proposes to classify and burden or release useful and necessary industries by popular vote is but a new *modus* of tyranny and oppression against which authentic manhood cannot fail to revolt.

10. A sound national policy would offer every just inducement to the youth of our free country to become owners of homes and tillers of the soil, their honest acres being held by a title as valid and respectable as that by which men hold ships, manufactories, and merchandise.

THE END.